Aura Christi

The God's Orbit

translated from Romanian by
Adam J. Sorkin and Petru Iamandi

The God's Orbit
Published in the United Kingdom in 2020

by Leslie Bell trading as Mica Press

47 Belle Vue Road, Wivenhoe, Colchester, Essex CO7 9LD
www.micapress.co.uk | books@micapress.co.uk

ISBN 978-1-869848-26-2

The God's Orbit
Poems copyright © Aura Christi, 2016
English Translation copyright © Adam J. Sorkin and Petru Iamandi 2020

The right of Aura Christi to be identified as the author of this work has been asserted by her in accordance with the Copyright, Designs and Patents Act of 1988.
All rights reserved.

I'm really grateful to my friends, Adam J. Sorkin and Petru Iamandi, for their inspired translation of my book, and the bright complicity incited in the ecstatic sky of poetry.

– Aura Christi

Poems in this collection have previously appeared in the literary journal *Poem* in the U.K. and *Apple Valley Review, Cider Press Review, National Translation Month, North of Oxford* and *Osiris* in the U.S.A.

Cast a knowing glance,
Your heart drunk
On love…

When there's no one
To talk with,
Write.

—George Bacovia

Table of Contents

Like the Sounds of a Many-Voiced Cry	1
The Fever	2
Someone Else's House	3
The Evening Is Only a House	4
The Earth Settles in Layers	5
Fear Is a Sign that the God Breathes	6
The Ferryman of Souls	7
The Kingdom	9
Oh, Consummate Suffering	10
Absolution	11
Divine Game	12
Spell	13
Like an Angel too Big	14
Porfiry Petrovitch's Lesson	15
Everything's Quiet	17
Elegy	18
Calligraphies	19
What Clumsiness of Heart	20
The Psalm of Light	21
Oh, Morning, Pure Accident	22
Midsummer Hour's Heat	23
Beauty, the Soul's Anchor	24
Autumn Has Come	26
An Ecstatic History	27
The God's Orbit	28
The Fire Child	29
How Can They Stand It?	31
Delphi	32
A Drawing in the Waters	33
Steps in October	34
The Liberating God	35
A Hunt for Snowflakes	37
Biblical	38
A Quasi-Descriptive Poem	39

It's Cold in the Orbit	40
No-Man's Land	41
Open Your Eyes	42
Dawn	43
Within the Range of Passionate Martins	44
So the Gods Come Down to Us	45
Thales' Dream	46
Dim Sight	47
Heraclitus	48
I Don't Know Why	49
The Birch Tree Park	50
Be a Sun	51
The Seventh Day	52
The Only Way	53
The Story of My Foreignness	54
The Dove in the Temple	56
Like Pieces of Osiris	58
White Apocalypse	59
Prince Myshkin's Smile	60
At Joseph Brodsky's Grave	61
Don't Be Afraid	63
Orbita zeului (the title poem in Romanian)	64
About the author	65
About the translators	66

Like the Sounds of a Many-Voiced Cry

It's as if you're living under a bell
with its mouth downward,
the lip of which you cannot find,
although you've been seeking it for a long time.
You're surrounded by a cottony,
misty light
that has rustled continuously for millennia…
At a certain moment,
deaf and dumb, you descend
step by step
into the cave deep inside you,
into the living, lingering light.

It's as if you're advancing under a bell
with its mouth toward the sky.
No one's there. No one at all.
Everything's fine. It couldn't be better.
The pitch dark is like amniotic fluid.
You guzzle down the loneliness of the other,
the other being you yourself, the stranger.
Then you describe the way in which you pause:
as was written in a book.
Someone inside you, appalled, keeps waiting.
Waiting to see how someone else
begins to ring both bells.
His iron hand booms in the air,
like the sounds of a many-voiced cry
far, far, far away.

The Fever

Evening. Torrid, stifling air.
Mars is going to rise before us soon.
Fever. The feeling that you're chewing sand.
Fragments of apocalypse deliriously crushed
under the eyelashes, like nutmeats between your teeth.
Overcome by torpor and astonishment,
the angels sing on the pyres, full of grace.
The gods are drowsy. Empty. The sky just a syllable.
A void, or not even that.

Once in a while: a breath of wind
sent by someone, like a sigh
coming from who knows where, cornered by death.
Everything gets confused, tangled together
far from good, from evil.
The air unbreathable. Here one lives
as if it's death. Run and hide.
Your world, God? A jungle
where one can't breathe. Or not even that.

Someone Else's House

But maybe everything is infinitely simpler.
Maybe we're only someone else's house –
a strange house that moves here and there,
without being able to turn into something else,

other than in sleep, in the dreams you forget
as soon as you awaken at dawn
and, holding your breath, watch how the sun
hesitates to rise, as though

someone awakened into life after the death of a creature
inside him, afraid to take his first steps,
found himself again like a strange house, ever steadfast,
to which he's always felt a connection.

Indeed, as if we were an unforgettable house, a lonely
house, like a pyre in the dead of night made
by someone who was lost. And since we don't know
who made it or if we'll eventually know

– hostages of being, friends of uncertainty –
we live as if we're floating to the land of fear
that knows, feels, sees everything and tells us what
we need to know. Tell me, God, whose transient flesh am I?

The Evening Is Only a House

It's like when you grasp your own meaning,
take fright and withdraw into yourself,
an obstinate creature, as into a huge crypt
invaded by the tolling of bells.
The evening brushes by you in passing
and goes on its way, without leaving
a single sign or trace.
Something inside you understands
the tolling of bells is
a rustle of wings,
the evening is only a house
that belongs to someone bigger and more powerful,
who passes by here…
While you're no more than the sign
of a stranger, known as if
in another life
where you were someone else's dream
or nothing more than a word –
mist rising from the Water of Life.
Who will listen? Who will presume to know?
…Maybe, yes, you're the sign
of a stranger or a word
hidden from time to time
between the roomy walls of your flesh,
like bats in a tomb.

The Earth Settles in Layers

It's all right, I kept telling myself. And the earth kept
settling in quiet layers over me.
I wasn't scared at all. I caught myself
waiting for the light to come

and put an end to my story.
Sometimes an indefinite terror suddenly
gaped wide like a chasm. I knew
it was a sign a visitor had brought

to herald something less frightful
than all that happened to me since I've been running
through this endless valley which, almost as a quirk,
others call *life*, though it resembles a wild circle.

Put everything that's happened between parentheses,
a friend advises me. So I keep quiet. Listen. Look.
I understand I can no longer muster the strength
                                    to pull myself together
and complete what I've always been asked to undertake.

How could I frame everything between parentheses?
This is my life, together with death's gestures.
I don't know if I'll have another
in this same land of being, far away.

Fear Is a Sign that the God Breathes

Just do something about this fear!
Look at it, it comes in flocks, God, like the late crows
on the threshold of winter. I listen to the caverns murmur inside me
and I know only that I no longer understand anything,
and you, after you showed yourself to me, won't come again.

In fact, no one has ever promised me
that I'd understand anything. Understanding appears like a fire
in fog, I tell myself. And I can hear how wonder fills
my chest as if I'd been saved
from the assault of a most atrocious game

that I can't find a name for, no purpose is revealed
to me either, although I wait for it to arrive
as spring arrives after an endless winter, and I feel that the fear
emerged out of nowhere is a sign that the god I dreamt of
last night breathes through me.

The Ferryman of Souls

"Take a step forward. Remember
you're a woman!" –
a man kept shouting
at the top of his lungs…
As if from another life
he kept shouting. A life left behind
as you might throw away an old coat…
What a shout, it stirs up the ashes.
In their crater something roars endlessly,
Then smoulders.

Glory be to the fire. Glory be to perdition.
And to the pain that tears me apart
– to the end of time – glory.
Glory to the cave in which
I stay like a lost Eve, belated,
a coiled snake
lying on a warm rock.
I'm a living being,
a sort of child of light,
a bastard of the bitter dark.
On my way to the land of perfection –
a tall son, lost.

I sit on this gentle shore:
neither man nor woman.
That man
keeps hunting me.
Yes. I'm the prey.
Oh God, the ferryman of souls
asks me for silver coins. There he is.
Throughout my life
I've paid in blood for everything.

I'm alive.
I smell of paper
and blackcurrants.
Like the dolphins in the water
I glide from one kind of waiting to another;
what do they call the never-ending one,
I wonder?

It roars, roars in my brain,
something that can't be found.
I go beyond a limit;
I rest my soul on another.
Like the cut-off head described
by the pestilence called Myshkin,
I know everything. Yes, everything.
The impossible?
A door opens
to a silence that
fills me with the tolling
of all the bells.

The Kingdom

What mean deity has founded a kingdom inside me?
Oh ho, the same body – the ancient arena of battle,
where armies of fear keep coming to blows
like beasts on a precipitous ridge…

Suffering gets monstrous, I say. Out of its ruins
I rose, not knowing why, until…
Love life like you love its nonsensical guides –
I repeat, a cuckoo thrown into someone else's nest, waiting.

But what's to be seen in this nest? Quietude?
Waiting, like a snake buoyed by the wave of salt?
What a rumble, what a roar, what a howl. Death is alive, it's everywhere.
In the middle of life – the same deep suffering.

Oh, Consummate Suffering

Oh, consummate suffering, smile
of the depths, contemplated each time
you stare eye to eye with God;
water of life, bread or no more than
a hesitation of the gods fallen into thought;
streambed of being, vapour of the soul, seal
or nectar of the untasted wine,
divine dash to the genius to be,
dew of a creature whose homeland
will never be here, but of this
incredibly slow afternoon,
from a breath that's reached its zenith –
how you're reinventing me, oh infinite suffering!
Breeze from the great unknown,
without my asking you, you give birth to me, at last.

Unheard-of haven of despondency,
uncharted island, familiar country,
unhoped-for homeland, where any attempt
to understand, any desire and breath seem
nothing more than a messenger of the brazenness
of staying alive, or a defiance of the being
who wants only to reach
for the last time the ultimate border
that separates it from the divine second,
when it recognises itself in the fresh green of the leaves,
in a lonely wingbeat
of someone unseen, crushed between eyelids,
in the fanning breeze of the wind that sculpts the hands
of a passer-by invoked night and day,
in the teardrop of the angel fallen from the milky dark
and in the barely recognisable roses.

Absolution

Quite beside yourself you watched
how someone changed
the caves of your ghost into extensive
hunting grounds.
As you found there
one gold mine after another,
you felt Death's fangs
strike into your nape
ever deeper, ever more savage,
with a subtle tenderness
disguised to seem clumsiness.
The edge? A tattered flag
in a lost battle,
maybe another game,
let's-play-infinity.
You can't help shuddering, can you?
Death is great,
you kept saying, seized
with a strange fever,
snatching the god out of the trees,
butterflies, grass, scents,
cornered by an illness
you couldn't find a name for
until, oh Lord,
as in another world,
crazily,
sublimely,
it snowed and snowed

Divine Game

Justice was delivered long ago.
On our bent, tender dolphin-like backs we carry
the heavy air, the joy of being –
a terrible sigh of the god undreamt of
by the Delphic giants.

From the ancient, dusty forms
I chose the circle. Or rather the circle
chose us for reasons that it alone knew.
We were running, dreaming as in a never-ending
divine game, dictated by stalactites.

Ever more lonely we were running,
we were floating, more powerful, more beautiful, it seems,
away from truth, from justice, carved
from living rock, among shells, algae, stones
or colossi repatriated into the wilderness.

Spell

Whose suffering
has built its nest in me
and doesn't want to leave
or stay?

What deity screams
its grief through my body,
terrible beauty,
feverish quadriga?

What rumble swirls,
roars, grows, struggles
like a bird caught
between life and death?

Like an Angel too Big

Stop. Stop shouting.
Anyway, no one can hear you.
Make the effort, pull yourself together, like late
autumn in leaves, like hands – in prayer.
Remember: the body is merely memory,
someone's unimaginable imprint
found again in the living stream of the world's childhood
about which you may never know anything.

The hell that burned you to ashes is far away.
You only need to take the first step
on this monotonous plateau called the Roof of the World.
Spread your arms wide. Fill your lungs with air
and breathe like a strip of land between waters.
"The time has come," the Tibetan monk says,
touching you, like an angel too big with its wing,
at the temple entrance. Your hour is near.

Porfiry Petrovitch's Lesson

That's it. I've reached perfection:
I live in a sphere of ivy.
Oh, what bustle, what fabulous hubbub can be found here!
You pulled me out of Hell's clutches, God.
Like an owl among ruins,
on the edge of the body I breathed a while.
Finally, I bolted.
I'm far from the body.
More than seven seas, seven countries away.
And I'm running. I keep running.

I've left the body behind.
It fattens grief; I spoil
and praise it in erudite treatises, chewed
by acarids, read by the wind, exotic plants…
It is the innocent lamb, ready. The stupefied lamb.
Yes. The body – the guinea pig, sailing
on rivers of blood.
I've shed my body,
my past – like a coat.
I've torn myself away from what was my land,
strange anchor in a world
that remained strange, distant.
Yes. The body – a chasm into which
I used to dive like dolphins.
On my day's agenda
thrown into the fire: the same body –
stranger than strangers.

I said yes to suffering.
To torture, death, the pit
and perdition I said yes.
And I took to my heels.

I said yes to hell, to illness,
to its consummate din.
For centuries I've been prostrating myself
before its altars.
It's been a long time since I was born
from something else.

Yes. Darkness defeated me.
Glory, glory, glory to you, God,
I belt out.
And run biting the dust:
I – the nuisance, the catastrophe,
the alien, the outlaw, the foreigner.
I'm running, no idea where.
My destination is running in itself;
running and silence free
ancient plants from blocks of anthracite.
Whose rhythm am I following, listening to?
What law secretes its nectar in me?

I press myself against my Rottweiler,
Count: my companion through Inferno,
my friend that grazes on my crocuses.
One breath as short as a syllable
and we'll touch the sky.
I said yes
to the Holy Ghost
of Life.
Amen.
Period.

Everything's Quiet

The rain was quick, more like a shower,
and killed the heat all at once;
one salvo I was about to say. Everything's quiet
and somehow finished. To live day by day
and to call whatever happens simple:
life, while life is too far,
somewhere one cannot reach in a flash.

But where exactly? you keep wondering and descend
deeper and deeper inside;
and you start to see everything with a transformed clarity:
the high sky, crystalline, the summer day, your hands
like nations of hands. You descend ever more slowly
until you recognise the road that is you yourself,
or someone forgotten by the centuries, who…

Elegy

The summer fades away like in a dream, everywhere.
You feel something in your eyes has faded.
You look at yourself in the mirror and listen to your humming:
I no longer am; I, I no longer am.
Everything's strange, lost and distant.
No one's around, yet something trembles;
something unseen seems to float like a wing,
brushing softly against you.
No one's around, you keep repeating, no one at all.
But then why is the air filling
with something impossible and heavy?
The darkness grows bewilderingly;
soon it will fall everywhere
to make its nest in hands, icons,
the hourglass, eyes.

Between the sky and you there's one syllable
of a forgotten verb from a dead language.
Not a big deal. Just wait. It's night.
Your room fills with something obscure
that reminds you of who you used to be
in another life, maybe; everything's strange, draped
over the surface of the being, distant, so very far.
The days get shorter, as they're supposed to.
The seconds stretch longer, night's perfume is strong
and the being – reduced to heart, eyes, breath.
Whose face is gathering itself, suddenly to be revealed?

Calligraphies

It's so still, as if
I've awakened in another world.
But maybe, overnight,
someone has changed my essence.
The storms are distant.
I stand on the threshold of my house
and the air is ever more fulfilled.
The beating of wings intensifies
when the anonymous calligrapher
paints lightning at sunset.

It's so still, I can hear
the seconds fall,
the colours in them twisting –
globes of nectar.
An abundance of light
spreads across my soul.
Legends, memories, wars
leaf through us, like a book.
Everything gets settled,
somehow has reached its climax,
when roses hardly tremble
in the breeze from who knows where
whispering, as in a dream,
the same divine epitaph:
"Roses – pure contradiction;
may no one sleep
under so many eyelids."

It's so still, you can hear
as in another life
how the world appears again
from the breathing of stone flowers.
Pushing with their muzzles
horses drive the fillies to water.

What Clumsiness of Heart

And it was evening. And in my soul
overwhelmed with quiet and great sadness
there was light: our comprehension is
like that of the blind who feel their way in the dark
and now and then search for their soul on the pyres.
But this is a story with roots
driven deep in the Achaean past, when they knew
life was a sort of trunk of being
pressed against itself, like nectar,
in late autumn, in the grapes.

Life is a sign of the god's presence.
At bottom the blood has understood
what I could not grasp
with my mind, a lonely man locked
in the wild circle of life, like in a heresy
that rouses passion – tent of our despair,
its root flowing into myth.
Life is a shelter for the god; yes, life is a nest
of being, a drive shaft of the world marked by a smile.
Life is the boundary of non-being in which
someone has snowed; oh, how much snow!

"What clumsiness of heart this night,
fallen on its muzzle like a divine animal,"
my daimon declares and inhales sharply
into its chest of grass or granite.

The Psalm of Light

How can I live, oh, God, with Your light,
if it strikes my entire being like a hatchet?
It's as though the world has grown a thousandfold
and you now can see like flowers or bees.
Like Prince Myshkin you suddenly could see.
These crazy, crazy colours,
who'd have the spirit to endure them?

Like the sublime Myshkin, I suddenly learned everything
About Your garden. In the morning it burned my eyes,
making me end in smoke and ashes. Colours, lines, sounds,
roses unearthing a revived pattern unexpectedly
from which a remarkable world started to swirl.
Hardly breathing, out of my oldest fears
someone arose on tiptoe.

How can I live, oh, God, with Your light?

Oh, Morning, Pure Accident

Oh, morning, pure accident –
the being's house, spur to completion!
And this insane hurry, breathless,
to-and-fro, between you and me.
Everything just to be, here and now;
yes, everything just to be beyond the essence of things,
beyond all measure,
with your ears pricked up to the blood
gurgling in the caverns; blood knows it all.
Indeed, the first to understand, to speak, and to keep quiet.
I'm its witness. The moon is witness –
the roar of the unseen that
brushed me with its muzzle in passing.

It is a sign, a message, a summons. Silence.
In its matrix: a beginning. Its time is come.
The colours – Eden's seal – throb in the statues.
Everything's a song, a boundary, an accomplishment, an element,
waiting on its ridge, and then – again a boundary,
a song and a greater loneliness
that feeds them all,
fulfilling itself in things.
Deep within their pulsing, there's something obscure,
that above all at evening supports the sky
gathered in these divine quince –
orbits of someone more lonely,
purer and too full to be now.

Midsummer Hour's Heat

The midsummer hour's heat, collapsed
into no one knows whose night and murmur,
on a country road – divine hand –
that splits the orchard in two and makes you
pull yourself together from a life turned strange…

Just as your body finds the time and patience
to get comfortable in a new coat,
you let yourself be consumed by something unusual
and so much alive, oh Lord, buried deep
inside, startled and groaning somewhere far away,

brought, drawn together, like lightning in a storm,
like the undamaged essence – in nectar,
like the being who knows everything – in the holy blood,
like the steam that brings us the saints from the icon
frames, like the indefinite sign

that makes John the Baptist
recognise – the first – Jesus,
like the order given at the gates of Jericho
to Blind Bartimaeus: "Take heart! Rise,
for He is calling you. Go to Him, be!"

Beauty, the Soul's Anchor

As much blood – that much faith;
as much faith – that much poetry,
he mumbled, the sleepwalker,
then he disappeared, leaving the sky behind
like the brave young heroes in fairy tales,
who, setting out for the world beyond to fight in,
made sure they left traces everywhere
so they'd know the way back
late at night the Fates had foretold.

Beauty is the soul's anchor,
he mumbled, the wandering son. Beauty
is the air between worlds. We, gathering
around him, gaping, as soon as we woke up
– vassals of habits – contradicted him,
defending our old nature, failed to agree,
made signs to each other, discreetly, kept teasing him,
"And the world that is, what could it be?"
"The world? Nothing more than a ghost,"
he answered, wrapping his cloak around him.
"Yes, the world is a sort of ancient pattern
that envelops us, the way the sky envelops the clouds,
the way the forest contains the asymmetrical oak
of my great grandmother, and the sea
– the dolphins – a sign that cherubs
are more than a mere tale,
and the planets – more than wonder,
and the houses – less than they appear."

"And we, what can we be?"
the crowd pressed him, sniggering
while trying to drive that useless lunatic –
without whom they felt they couldn't live – into a corner.

"We? What can we be? The progeny of chimeras
who have become the masters of
all the seen and the unseen,
who no longer differentiate between life and death
and who have invaded what you somehow
inappropriately call *reality*,
defeating it little by little,
especially when everything becomes
a perfect desert."

"We hardly understand a word,"
whispered a clever someone in the confused
crowd. But the lunatic raved on:
"The gods are living patterns, memories
of the world's childhood.
The wells – orbits of someone too lonely
to be born in any other form.
The grass is a sign that we can always
become the stems of flowers, cranes, petunias,
tongues of fire or fingers of terrible angels
who remember once in a while
that cicadas sing only in sleep.
We are the song of someone
who wants never to be awakened
and who for centuries has been singing
and praying even while asleep."

Autumn Has Come

A night fallen on its muzzle, like a cringing animal.
Autumn has come. I suddenly shrink inside myself
and wait. I no longer know when I lived
and if ever I'll live again, God,
what dream, what life, what story I'll awaken in,
if the same room, on the same day,

among books, prayers and simple pencils,
muttering all sorts of things,
among letters, groans, icons, planets, flowers
and barely grasped words. All things become almost simple
as I wait on their edge for something to happen.

When I understood that death didn't exist
it was late in the eternal lateness,
and my brother – my nearest kin – never appeared again.
Meanwhile autumn had come to the sky too.
Yes, it's autumn, everywhere; and I haven't died.

It's important to keep waiting. Someone, some time, will show up
to take me away from here. As if from another world,
what a terrible autumn God has made for us.
The heart knows everything, yes, everything, and tells
what's proper to know only to those who in former days were
birds carved in bronze, air, memories, a rainbow.

An Ecstatic History

I'm standing at the open window
and yearning after my incredible life
as if it were a strange heresy.
In that ecstatic history
– of a mathematical exactitude –
my body, oh ho! remained somewhere behind,
like a tree without leaves, glimpsed
from a speeding car; yes, a lone tree
on the crest of the hill, like a story
I heard in my childhood, completely forgotten
and – out of the blue – climbing violently
to nature's surface, unaccountable.
like my Father's death.

It's autumn. Everything looks round, full.
Rust, death and gold have made a nest in the leaves.
Everything seems at its end. Forever. And how enormous
the afternoon is! The light that has reached the summit is ready to die.
Overripe angels plummet down from the sky as though
they were gathered from a myth half-known
or even less, along with the gods, the past, the precision,
the mist, the homeland and their steadfast serenity.

To live like migratory birds,
as if you bade good-bye to everything;
yes, to burn – like the birds – thoroughly and
to change whatever you touch into light and flame,
I say. And I tremble. Yes, tremble.
(Matter lost in an ecstasy absorbing thought;
illness, a garden, roses, suffering, falling, limits,
the desert, an atrocious handicap – the realm of becoming.)
And I miss terribly
my incredible life, God,
in which Your illimitable hand, exact and gentle,
brought death to my face.

The God's Orbit

Everything was ripe and so late,
somehow reaching the summit.
At last I had learned to choose eternity
from transitory things,
just the way you sift wheat from chaff,
the way the flesh falls from the bone, the bone –
from the marrow, and the soldier – from his weapon.
This autumn is nearly ripe. Midnight,
mid-thought. The horizon drinks from the sea.

Give me a name for the self-pride, the rock
or the eye from which the sun first rose,
like the gods from myth. Give me a name
for the one who carved the man from clay,
and the woman – from his melodious rib,
making her long for that obscure house.
Give me a name for the humility
that revives the world and teaches me how to endure
this sharp, immense light.

As usual, I wait. I wait for autumn's
sweet scent to calm me
late at night, when wings beat and the sky
whirls about, the colours – the air of the eyes, the roses,
the Lares, the ever more watchful peaks
that propel me
toward the unknown god's orbit –
primordial,
heretic strangeness.

The Fire Child

God, I wished so hard
to reach you out of death!
I trembled, burned, died and came to life
in an instant, falling back for no apparent reason
into that childish way of being, as when – erupting
from the depths of the water – you desperately
grab hold of a life-ring.
Everything was exactly as in former times
– yes, in another life – when I felt
the sea closer and closer:
its smells subdued me, travelled through my being and soul,
stirring them from the depths, as the plough
in early spring turns one furrow
over another, bigger and blacker.

When it was very late, when lateness
seemed to have reached its end point, I understood
in all that history I was neither the aim
nor the target. There was someone else involved, I once called him
the stranger, the fire child, the heathen…
I'm but an instrument
in this crazy game which, oh God,
I understand less and less, but maybe
I don't even need to understand;
for everything is far from comprehension.
I need only remain pure and wait.
To descend within, deeper and deeper, and not question anything.
To entrust myself entirely to that mystic nameless whirlpool.
There, faraway – in the intimate abyss –
to listen to my blood. To follow blindly
the words that come to me I don't know where from
until I am no longer myself, until all that I am
comes to dust;

then, out of the dust someone begins to put together
a sort of cradle, earth, sanctuary, maybe a throne,
or a shrine for something greater and more powerful
that brings me other words
which I write down most neatly
– in a cold, exact light –
far from evil and good,
far from all that's on the surface,
where I am kept
alive by that fire child.

How Can They Stand It?

How can I stand it? I spoke aloud
the barely audible question
and thought of the springs
that draw sap, fish, salt,
wave and abyss from the sea.

I searched for the shadow in which
they said I existed.
And I saw only an enormous
light, then the same smile
of an actor lonely and sad

among heresies and heaps of flowers…
How can you stand it? they kept asking me.
I couldn't figure out the awkwardness, the error
or the genius of always being late
in the abyss of the same myth

where asking such a question
is like asking someone
how they bear the snow,
how history can tolerate its heroes
and the ocean its waves, its sharks and shells?

How can the saints stand their icons,
the endless alley its melodious pines,
their flight the eagles? How can the Aegean Sea
bear the earth – the sole of the foot
and the legends?

How does the air stand the birds,
the apples the apple-tree, the wild flowers the forest,
the road the traveller's steps, the jungle the tigers,
the greatest of all sages the sunrise,
and the divine Olympus the city of gods?

Delphi

Apollo appears between the columns,
descends step by step,
supports the sky with one hand
and the wise axle of night.

Hera watches over the snakes of the olive tree.
Zeus stares up at the ridges.
Look, there's another beginning in store for us
in the remote garden that's falling asleep

and waiting for the gods to arrive on horseback
in the chill startling the morning,
balanced on the backs of the slender dolphins
who are going to disperse the mist

from here, from Delphi – sublime city,
with its curved sky, held in the hands
of slender gods, led by Apollo
and flights of tender dolphins.

A Drawing in the Waters

The beautiful ghosts
– snowing under my eyelids –
come in my sleep
to water the Pegasuses.

Holiness draws its breath
in them,
like the sun in things,
slender gods and rings

hardly sketched
wild in the waters
by a hand of air
nearby, far away.

Under a spell to stay,
to wait, to listen.
Pressed against chimeras,
to run barefoot

on lawns of mint,
between sunrise and sunset,
in an eternal present,
lonely, of granite.

Steps in October

Death's serpent has been gone for centuries
and fall has suddenly grown from your temples.
The sun is at its highest; you carry it wistfully on your head
like an amphora. The leaves' Moirai
know what must follow.

Since you've come back from far away,
your garden smiles in briers,
October sets fire to pyres amidst the clouds,
playfully outflies the hawks

and fades away in the shadowless peace,
among mischievous quince, hard grapes,
by which we measure the distances between planets,
lovers and rainbows, roses and bumble-bees.

It's peaceful. The magnolia smiles in buds again.
The roughened grass climbs to the sky step by step...
The hours grow longer. The light is almost ripe and caresses
the colours' ghosts, too alive but slow.

And there seems to be no end of it.
Magic from everywhere subdues us.
The scents are celebrating. Autumn plucks us
out of ourselves and carries us on its
great, transparent wing.

The Liberating God

I'm in the air; oh ho, I recognise myself!
I keep saying as I try to tear myself away
from the sky that contains me,
like autumn's ghosts in day's amphora, alive.
I'm just the air's relief, liberated
from I don't know whose lungs and heart.
I die, revive in an instant, like Aurora's panthers
which, with a sudden leap, split dawn
into two asymmetrical halves,
with their wings of unseen metal,
then the lavender field blooming on the horizon,
and the sea, here mauve, there green and bluish.

The god comes head first and, ah, everything
changes into more than a story.
Yes, everything becomes much more than it is.
What one can see is the kingdom
of all that the horses, ladybirds,
butterflies, grass and people have never seen.
It depends on the light in which you dream.
It depends which tiger you fall asleep on
and which eagle's gaze you wake up in.
Everything else is no more than murmur, mist,
or no more than a line
written by someone in water.
The rest is only a silence, changed into gods,
things, lovers, wasps, beavers, frigates.
The rest is only a vast greenish glance
encompassing us all

and is equal – second by second –
to itself. I am not equal to myself.
The sky is not equal to itself.
The earth is not equal to what it is.
People are more than the signs

of the most beautiful worlds of dream.
My guardian angel is equal to wonder –
the body of an empire carried on their wings
by flights of bees and seagulls.
The grass is something more than it seems.
And the birds, ah, the birds are a kind
of lily of the air, dreamed by sea
creatures – temple of tragic stars set long ago.

There's an angel trembling in every thing.
A song asleep in every angel.
The god comes, builds a temple in you,
then makes himself a shrine from eagles, words
and the bones of unknown heroes,
lighting up the dim sky.
Then unexpectedly he promises you to another world
and – without bringing you tidings –
departs, together with horses, women,
monks, sand martins,
rock butterflies
and priests in palanquins.
On his right shoulder he carries
the olive tree mountains,
on his left –
the littlest stars.

You remain alone and empty
with that strange altar between your ribs;
you can hardly breathe, defeated by the memory
of a world that isn't yours:
a world born from the temple
of the liberating god,
moulded by the thought of some unknown being –
a shore sparkling between the waters,
near, near, so very near,
under the sky – the dome of a church
watched over by hysterical seagulls.

A Hunt for Snowflakes

Colours are the masks of someone
lonelier and sadder.
He who built the eye and the temple knows
the night's bed when it slowly leans
toward light's living heart.

Trees are metal columns,
half-hidden in the sky.
He who has made the thought and the hand
knows the secret place where
for millennia his origin has been

the core, the nectar, the nature of things
and the cold, candid whiteness of the moon.
It's autumn; the quiet is complete
amidst the leaves, seas, people and shells.
What a feverish night, like a crypt,

its shadow twisted in the lake's ghost,
with living water lilies and late dragonflies
that try the waters' strength.
What a song takes form from the depths
and carries away the darkness, collapsed into a boat.

He who has been fettered in light, like the sun in its orbit,
like the bones – in the body, like an axle – in thought,
from all that we are, knows what has collapsed into eternity
and which hemisphere belongs to the autumn, death,
sky and day trapped in the transparent hourglass

by the same hand that realises when life is
a hunt and when we are, oh, no more than
children who, seeing the first snow, catch
with their eyes, mouths and hands snowflake after snowflake that fly
and fall, pale with cold, as hosts from the misting sky.

Biblical

Autumn, sublime prophesy
exploring wells, forests, colours,
it's an uncertain end that blows gently
from the leafless crown
of the oak, reflected in the sky
and the sounds bowed from holy violins.

Autumn, sublime prophesy, overflowing
the riverbeds, birds, meteors,
a beginning in everything seems about to be.
The bare earth is also the darkness, much too gentle.
And the light that blazes its trail is good,
leaving hints and traces everywhere, too alive

to appear suddenly under the empty sky.
The condors can't be seen in the book of the horizon.
In everything the wait groans faintly, erupting
unawares like a pre-thought from the spirit
that has been our foundation
ever since the eve of Genesis.

He is too lonely to die, too lonely
to be on this earth with his heart scarcely beating
under the small legs of the divine dove
which carries in its beak the little olive branch
and stands face to face, eye to eye,
soul to soul, with its only Neighbour.

A Quasi-Descriptive Poem

It's so cold that ghosts and locust trees shiver
under the darkened sky like rotten quince.
Fog throws its cloak over things,
you can hardly see three steps ahead; it caresses the spiders
dropping precious stones in no-one's web.

It's day one and we are at the crossroads
travelled by proud herons and pheasants.
The ever sparser foliage has exiled all its green
onto the moss in the well, along which
two stray crickets bear their crosses like Mohicans.

It's so quiet, like the end of the world.
The fire and the road search the orchard.
Just before daybreak the heavenly bodies fall toward Hypnos.
The sea gathers its soul in pearls, shells and foam.
The lambs, too young, are about to fall off the mane of the seconds.

Almost everywhere a beginning makes its nest.
Aged dragons spit fire and nestle in the leaves,
then have second thoughts and return
hand in hand with mysterious archangels
who invite them to go harvesting medusas.

It's Cold in the Orbit

Like the light in churches
the profane seagulls rise
in circles, lulling to sleep
my sadness, my mistakes, my years,

in the morning, when the sun is up.
Eternity arises and grows from images
in relief, and things that have been studying
their being for ages in the holy

pages of the history of the Earth,
since its beginning carried
on the bronze blood of the saints
and never-to-be-forgotten shadows,

revived by haughty, absent-minded gods
in the years of fire when, righteously, they rode about
through the passions of time,
under the unredeemed sky,

and through such cold that parents keep silent in icons,
a cold such that you forget your name;
you shiver and – singing –
pay your last duties.

It's colder and colder in the orbit;
let's be like roses and love like them.
Desperate birches catch fire and burn
under the vault of my thoughts.

No-Man's Land

Darkness – a no-man's land
that cries its sadness
at every street corner.
What you touch forgets you, grows copiously
in everyone's soul of fire
and defeats you very seldom, but incontestably.

The second day rises from chimeras
that support the earth on four elephants,
as really happened in antiquity
when we heard the world's heart throb,
kept by Apollo in melancholy spheres,
then in his temple built by sprites.

Everything begins with unwritten laws
in the maternal womb of all things.
Everything revives from water, air, the fire
tended by three goddesses: Clotho, Lachesis
and the adamant Atropos – sublime graces of fear
who, oh ho, knew almost all there is to know.

Open Your Eyes

Open your eyes wide, keep them open.
Don't forget to breathe. No matter what,
inhale deeply and don't ask:
until when, why and how, how come?
I'm with you, walled in the column of the second.
I'm with you as no one has been nor ever will be
with someone. In a not-yet-begun peace, someday

you'll sing, sweet abstractions, with earrings,
liana bracelets, laurel rings and brown sandals,
dear beings gathered at dawn from the only tree:
everything can be seen. Aurora passed mounted on a cloud
and I winnowed light from darkness, the waters from the land.
And it was so cold the birds stopped flying.
And it was hot under the morning's vault, alive.

The third day arrived, curved like an arch. And a breeze
started to blow over the seen and the unseen.
And then loneliness was created – the matrix of being.
And very late, when we had only
one breath to breathe, dearest chimeras, life was created
from everything that hadn't been seen before: suffering, waiting,
mist, rib and whatever else could be found in a handful of clay.

Dawn

The light sends its ambassadors to the birches,
forgets its fires in the roses and the sunset.
It's evening even in words; you rock the archangels.
The world somehow appears finished.

The dawn waits to form you
while Atropos sharpens her scissors.
You saw the boundary between people and the law
while the Fates sank deep into their own thought.

The trees have taken their shadows to pasture.
All things breathe a dull waiting.
The garden gathers its richness of beauties
and laughs in the colt that frisks about

after butterflies, field rabbits and wasps.
When peace set loose its offspring, it counted them in the sun
and drank the dew from the stag's crown,
I separated night from day and,

to my utter surprise, in the candid spheres
of the afternoon floated as in a dream, slowly, singing,
feverish beings, nightingales lonely
as soon as they took shape and mind.

Within the Range of Passionate Martins

Your country, the long awaited land,
lies within the range of passionate martins.
From the middle of the roses, in their fragrance, you take shape
and dream in the trees of the last century.

A few more steps and you'll approach
the original trunk.
Close your eyes, sleep sheltered by bustards,
inside their inviting circle.

Close your eyes, sleep, enter
under the stranger's eyelid.
Trust the evening hours
caved in on no-one's orbit

from the country of the pious martins
where you can see everything through people, where
from great distances you face death in eagles, take form
and revive in ecumenical seconds.

So the Gods Come Down to Us

So the gods come down to us;
November sends us messages from everywhere:
it all seems slowly to come to an end…
They walk single file through the void
inhabited by shy trees and leaves
fallen into the sky's grass, redeemed.

The firmament is heavy and the mountains high like the sea,
the heavy hour lies in the rarefied air
and in forums lit from the underground.
You walk alone. Your eyes are too heavy.
The wish to die unearths in everyone
secrets forgotten over the centuries.

The wind drives us to a new conclusion,
with the autumn gathered in eyes, hourglasses,
stones. Oh Lord, how many times
has the soul locked itself in briers, separate,
like the sun in the quince with its face touched
by the gods at dawn, when they come down to us?

Thales' Dream

The gods walked through fog and tornadoes.
I stood face to face with the chimera.
I could see its crease bend and fall;
just as Hera falls into dream and jealousy

when sly Zeus looks for his counterpart
among olive trees and righteous swallows.
Take a look – the twilight has pricked up its ears
in cypresses, wells and lazy orbits.

Everything looks so clear.
The chimera's eyes grow greener and greener.
Thales returns to the happy water
through which you can see all things.

In the beginning was the Water of Life,
the gods mumble sadly, cloaks in their hands;
the bronze they were cast in knows
when Zeus shows himself in its delicate mistress.

Tremendous havoc lies in store for us,
twisting the multiple into its only bundle.
Melancholy gods float at dawn and watch:
everything begins from the same body.

Dim Sight

It's autumn for the angels, beneath the waters,
and I can hardly remember
the tree from which I plucked this word
and where its sweet syllables celebrate,
wandering from ridge to ridge.

What do you call the bird
that hatched it, discreetly withdrawn?
Where could its country be, its hesitating
sky, its story, maybe its clay
and its last nest?

Ah, time passes, the way pedigree dogs
follow their masters at the hunt.
The seconds arch the same way
the manes breathe: deeply, in haste,
like eagles slicing the alpine sky into strips.

I pluck myself from myself; I turn my head
to that autumn of long ago;
I can barely make out the tree of life, the animals,
the priests deep in sleep, lost in their coats of mail.
And I hear the rush of a heavenly body.

Heraclitus

I did right by the birds.
I built a slender vault to the white sky.
But then, why does sadness overwhelm me,
when the night's eyes open in the grass,
wells and seas, and before it is too late, in everyone?

I did right by the bears, the lions, the deer
and gathered the trees, the aurochs and the plants in my hands;
it was the first forest in this world. But then,
why do I lock myself in sleep, like the dead in the earth,
and like the ancient silences – in babies?

You, hesitating, late, when the evening
flashed quietly and frightfully at sunset,
from Adam's rib, singing, I carved you. But then,
why do you disturb my peace? What have you found in that shriek?
How far away do you go on flowing, from its mouth?

I Don't Know Why

I don't know why I try so hard to defend myself against beginnings.
I wait for my heart's amphora to fill very gradually.
All the springs start to flow from the mud trodden
by the flying angels who, poked in the ribs
by something indefinite, have learned to wander both

night and day, unhindered, amid people
until they tame them and befriend them,
then, after a long time, when they're worn out,
they seem to pick one at random and in their body
draw breath for an entire year.

Then some of them withdraw only they know where,
leaving no traces, no signs nor hostages,
and wait for their heart's amphora to fill
and spill beyond the brim. In the meantime,
they try to defend themselves against another beginning.

The Birch Tree Park

They've retreated into the leaves
And to the spring where
all the blackbirds return, no matter how late
it is and how many alleys and pathways
of the yellow birch tree park you follow.

They've retreated into the pavilion
with the deep well, dug long ago,
and make their way through spiders,
small branches, bees, grasshoppers, twigs,
but sometimes they fail to reach the water.

At dawn, the most beautiful would like to hide
in the wild rose garden, knowing that there,
at break of day, you go with hesitation.
Even then a few of them breathe their last.
Unknowingly you pass by invisible crosses.

There's a deafening shout coming from God knows where;
Later, November takes you on its great wings and carries you away,
then death's silences, confused, steal you from there.
Later, trembling, you close their mouths with your hand,
the way the day closes the dark in the hollow.

Be a Sun

Inside us the secret keeps digging roads.
Be a sun and rise without fear. Dawn comes
at the hardest of times: imperially, definitively, naturally.
A blood relative, the moon carves sculptures of water

and hangs its crown from the forested sphere
so that you can be. Come, raise yourself up from heaven's colours
and listen to the unicorn – the chosen among the chosen flowers –
and be a moon, rise from the waters and the leaden air of the crypt.

Thousands of beings tend each other in hidden places
in the garden and draw their breath in the dark,
when its whisper ascends from the ground to the ankle
and becomes master of the grass, the temple, the sea,

dying without reason. Defeated, you again become a sun,
you rise from within as if from an abyss, wandering for centuries
and with difficulty assemble yourself from simple clay and the lakes.
November is at its zenith; only then, the late chills

make you live again. It's good, everything belongs to you,
rich man: the moon and the sun, the earth and the condors.
Peace gives words to apparitions, the kid-goats in the mill's corner,
when I knead you, I give you life, I look and see through you.

You cry, breathe through me, smile, and wonder.
As was written: the dough is worked in each of us.
Night and day, the world is reborn from magic and wonder,
prodded in the rib by the much too happy kid-goats.

The Seventh Day

The autumn transcribes ancient chronicles in the air
and briskly crosses a small bridge late at night.
With its cold fingers the wind sculpts
the bas-relief of the V of the forehead

and chooses people with autumn in their bodies.
The seventh day draws near to sunset.
Your gaze makes the blood rise to my cheeks, my temples
when I ask you, "What else have you been thinking about?"

You remain still. Leaves fall from the strange silence,
and the sky gathers its sadness in icons,
the wells sniff out their chill,
the path takes its soul to the skylight.

The entirety of autumn dresses in new vestments
as was written in the Holy Book long ago.
The light gathers the bards of old along the paths, in kiosks,
in parks, in the leap of fish, praised by a rock.

The Only Way

I've been thinking
of your deeds
and the wonders
given only to those
who cannot live
without them.
From your night
I rose
like a great noon
from smart rings,
drawn in the whirlpool
of icy waters.
August, contemplated
in contradictions,
suddenly revealing
the only way…
Among butterflies and roses,
rabbis of sweet scents
and sombre marigolds,
today your living hand
has rested.

The Story of My Foreignness

What am I? I asked the wind, the grass,
my guardian angel and then the night.
Where do I come from, where am I going?
I asked the eagle,
the little dove in the temple
and the ladybird and, much later,
an olive garden,
and the forgotten crater of a volcano,
inhabited by a sage. Never
have I received an answer.
Just icy silence;
like the silence of the beginning of the world,
of a slain daimon.

What am I, for all that, what *am* I?
I anxiously asked Mother
who – beyond any doubt –
had to know:
I am body and soul brought into this world
by her body and soul.
Sinking into thought she, my saint, smiled,
and, after a long pause, heard herself whisper,
"Can't you see how foreign you are?"
Light years separated us.
I stood under the red sign
of the most luminous star,
the miracle called Aldebaran.
I don't understand why I kept crying.
I didn't understand why
my foreignness was growing like a plant,
like a divine garden,
over the summer and the fall, over the mountain peaks,
eagles, goats and manes, horses and the grass,

toward new seas and new lands,
yes, it grew so fast, ever fatter,
prospering – oh glory to God, glory –
second by second, year by year.

And still, still: what am I?
I couldn't stop,
and I went on writing from Hell, with love,
I no longer could quiet.
I ran through the forests of my country
that were desperately felled, and I went on asking:
the evening, the paths, the aurochs, the wild boars,
the animals of the sky made of salt and dreams.
Later, back home, I asked
the towering oak tree in the neighbours' yard.
Oh, oak tree, this dear trunk
of God knows what deity,
with whom I now stand face to face,
who burns my heart,
burns my eyes,
burns my soul, yes, the oak tree –
the mark of my melancholy –
it was so sad, so proud
and quieter than a hawk.

Then, when the remoteness began
to rot little by little,
in a half whisper I asked
the sea, my lifelong friends
and, most especially, my enemies.
I bear witness:
I heard only the second's echo
that died in the excessive air
of those unforgettable questions
making – like the pharaohs – their tombs.

The Dove in the Temple

I found the climb excruciating.
The slope had become impossibly steep,
the light devouring,
when suddenly I entered the temple,
out of breath.
I shut my eyes tight.
I needed to get used
to the light inside there:
weak, almost dark.

I stood face to face with it:
I – a human creature,
like a tree stripped of leaves,
it – a bird,
like the anchor of someone
much more powerful
and much bigger.
I held my breath
for fear I might scare it.
It held its glance
suspended on my breath
like a liana, like an arm hanging
down from a tired body,
after making a superhuman
effort.

It tilted its small head
to one side, wondering,
and it stared at me.
Ah, how it stared at me,
then pecked
from a tray set
in the middle of the altar…

I remember how
the dove stared at me
and suddenly I knew,
I understood everything.
I remember
the thundering light
into which
I cast myself
as I left the temple.

Like Pieces of Osiris

Like pieces broken from Osiris –
these lines at the edge of the divine autumn…
I cannot measure my strength with them,
when I put myself together from steep climbs
in the barely recognisable body,

and I return to the matrix after long wanderings
for who knows what reasons, or until when.
I can barely see the wing that used to be my earth.
Oh, tender syncopes, sweet illusions
in the dirty, sacred air,

nothing's to be done; a world has to be made,
for *everything was so good*. A holy book of life,
death is nowhere to be found; I searched everywhere.
The god breathes through a broken wing,
like an animal fallen on its muzzle.

White Apocalypse

I didn't like the big cities,
neither the avenues nor the crowds.
I wasn't crazy about the sky's concrete.
Sometimes I was afraid of people, took
to my heels and fled the carbonised air.

Yes, I ran for my life
among butterflies, sweet cherry trees and roses
to hunt for old rhythms and much beloved scents.
I yearned for something impossible
whenever I stared at dew on my ankles.

I missed my Mother's astonished eyes
whenever I pointed to the moon, calling out, Do you see it?
Like people, just like us. The moon, my Mother told me,
has eyes, a mouth, a nose, eyebrows; her good fairy
will bring the deepest snows.

Strange, the next day it snowed as in the fairy tales.
Before long everything was covered by drifts as high
as a house. The trees were white, the roofs were white.
The giant beast of the white apocalypse swallowed us
in its cautious, stealthy rhythms.

Prince Myshkin's Smile

When there's nothing left to be saved,
if, however, you're stubborn and keep searching,
you have the chance to find a scrap, no matter how fragile,
grown from the smile of the counterfeit idiot Myshkin,
from the shout of a child.

And if you search for more, you can't miss it:
inside you there's an Abel as well as a Cain.
The terror of double thoughts gives you
no less trouble. Incredibly slowly, death
lowers the last flag to half-mast.

What a strange coincidence: only then
do you feel how, little by little, the waters are receding.
Only then do you find yourself anew, quite alone in the world.
Defeated among the defeated, as if from a bolgia
you see an immaculate mast fluttering at the horizon.

At Joseph Brodsky's Grave

Autumn is at its zenith; here I am, God,
in the murmur of the grass that sleeps
at the edge of the city cornered by the cold
and the wolves through which I howl my sadness.

Alone, under the ivy, I lure my ghost,
the darkness trapped in the sarcophagus,
shaded by pine trees for centuries, where I listen
to the silence bearing fruit in the lost distich.

Everything is as was written in the book.
From psalms, wars, dead histories,
through millennia, royal charters, your glance
flows and flows, gently, demiurge.

You're like the sea, you're like the fire,
you're like the sky with fortune in its favour,
in which we work – ghost within ghost –
lands, eyes, temples, air,

haze, sweet scent; through you
everything becomes rounded, without stain. Who
turns the ghost into an error
and the sky into a giant bird?

I rise from the rocks, melancholy.
In the gods' twilight, the autumn knows:
from hell the beauty founded to lie
sings with much love.

My sister, death, knows all.
Over the white peaks, in the living quiet,
a last smile in the book of life
blooms in the shadow of sadness…

It's you I miss, God. It's cold,
through storms and lagoons I cry my sadness aloud.
In this poem albatrosses build nests
under the eyelids of red roses.

In this poem, alone, through you
I wane, I light up, I darken,
I rise, I love, I am extinguished in everyone
and I slip away in the vanquished grass.

Don't Be Afraid

Don't be afraid, no matter what.
The grass is as green as ever.
Fallen into thoughts, the Pegasuses of light
leaf through you like a book

belatedly, as if they'd found
their peace in a house that has no master.
Don't be afraid. The autumn winks
with God knows whose eyes.

Everything is covered by the ashes of the years.
Overripe cherubs fall from the sky.
Fate hums. The time has come,
the iron band of this age breaks.

Don't be afraid. I'm here.
I wait for you in sweet scents, eagles, colours.
This country road is my hand,
trodden by you so many times.

Orbita zeului

Totul era copt şi-atât de târziu,
oarecum ajuns pe culme.
În sfârşit, învăţasem să aleg eternitatea
din fiecare de lucrurile trecătoare
cum se alege grâul de neghină,
carnea se desprinde de os, osul –
de măduvă, iar soldatul – de armă.
E toamnă dată în pârg. Miez de noapte,
miez de gând. Orizontul se-adapă din mare.

Daţi-mi un nume pentru orgoliul, piatra
sau ochiul, din care a răsărit pentru prima dată
soarele, ca zeii din mit. Daţi-mi un nume
pentru cel care a cioplit omul din lut,
iar femeia – din coasta-i melodioasă,
dându-i dorul de acea – obscură – casă.
Daţi-mi un nume pentru smerenia,
care renaşte lumea şi mă învaţă să sufăr
această lumină uriaşă, tăioasă.

Ca de obicei, aştept. Aştept miresmele
toamnei în mine să se aşeze
seara târziu, când aripi bat şi răscolesc
văzduhul, culorile – aerul ochilor, rozele,
larii, vârfurile tot mai treze,
care mă mână spre orbita
zeului necunoscut –
străinătate eretică,
de început.

About the author:

Aura Christi is a Romanian poet, novelist, essayist, journalist, and editor. Born on January 12, 1967, in Chişinău, the capital of The Republic of Moldova (the former Moldavian Soviet Socialist Republic), she graduated from the State University School of Journalism in 1990. In 1993 she received Romanian citizenship and settled in Bucharest, Romania's capital.

Christi's volumes of poetry, published in both Moldova and Romania, span two and a half decades of productivity. Her collections of new poems include *On the Other Side of the Shadow* (1993); *Against Me* (1995); *The Ceremony of Going Blind* (1996); *The Valley of Kings* (1996); *The Last Wall* (1999); *Northern Elegies* (2002); *Austere Gardens* (2010); *The Sphere of Cold* (2011); *The God's Orbit* (2016); and two novels in verse, *The Heart's Genius* (2017) and *The Island of the Resurrection* (2019).

Christi's novels include the four titles in the *Night Eagles* tetralogy: *The Sculptor* (2001, 2004); *The Stranger's Night* (2004, 2016); *The Great Games* (2006); *The Lambs' Snow* (2007). She has also published *The House in the Dark* (2008) and *The Wild Circle* (2010).

Her eleven books of essays include *Bits of Being* (1998); *Wine's Religion* (2007); *Three Thousand Signs* (2007); *Exercises in Destiny* (2007); *Nietzsche and the Great Noon* (2011); *Dostoyevsky–Nietzsche. The Eulogy of Suffering* (2013); *Home-in-Exile* (2016); and her latest, *From the Inferno, with Love* (2017).

In 2013, www.librariapentrutoti.ro and Ideea Europeană Publishing House initiated the Aura Christi Author Series in fifteen e-books, twelve of which have already appeared.

Christi's novels and essays deal primarily with human destinies under the yoke of foreign occupation, a recurrent leitmotif of hers, which she calls *at-home-in-exile*. They focus on geographic exile and the attempt to find a homeland in poetry.

Christi's poetry has been translated into sixteen languages: French, Russian, Swedish, Greek, Italian, Spanish, German, Polish, Hungarian, Macedonian, Chinese, Korean, Bulgarian, Albanian, Hebrew and English. She has travelled widely as a guest of literary festivals.

Aura Christi is editor-in-chief of *Contemporanul* ("The Contemporary") magazine, which modernises a journal that claims its founding in 1881 in the city of Iaşi in the northeast of Romania, and after a number of gaps, still continues today as a vital part of Romanian culture. She is member of both the Romanian Writers' Union and the Moldovan Writer Union.

Aura Christi has been honoured with many important literary prizes, among them T Romanian Academy Prize for Poetry (1996); The Romanian Writers' Union (199 and The Moldovan Writers' Union (1998) Prizes; Author of the Year fro The Association of Literary Publications and Publishing Houses of Roman (2007); the Poesis Prize(2008); The "Opera Omnia Prize for Poetry" of t Ronald Gasparic Romanian-Canadian Festival (2009); the Internation Nichita Stănescu Festival Prize (2017); and the Opera Omnia Silver Med in Tel Aviv (2019).

About the translators:

Adam J. Sorkin has published more than sixty books of Romani translation and won numerous awards including the Poetry Society (U.K Translation Prize, the Kenneth Rexroth Memorial Translation Prize, t Ioan Flora Translation Prize, and the Poesis Translation Prize, amo others. He has been granted Fulbright, Rockefeller Foundation, A Council of England, New York State Arts Council, Academy of Americ Poets, Soros Foundation, Romanian Cultural Institute, and U.S. Natior Endowment for the Arts support for his literary activity. His recent boo include *The Hunchbacks' Bus* by Nora Iuga, translated with Diana Mano (Fayetteville, NY: Bitter Oleander Press, 2016), which was longlisted f the National Translation Award in Poetry. In 2016 he also served as gue editor and main translator for a special Romanian double issue of t literary magazine *Poem* and for an issue of *Paragraphiti* featuring you Romanian poets. In 2017, Sorkin published *Syllables of Flesh* by Floar Țuțuianu, translated with Irma Giannetti (Washington, DC: Plamen Pre: with illustrations by Țuțuianu, who is also a visual artist, and *A Deafeni Silence* by Magda Cârneci, translated with Mădălina Bănucu and with t poet (Bristol: Shearsman Books). In 2018 Mircea Dinescu's *The Barbaria Return*, translated with Lidia Vianu, appeared from Bloodaxe Books (Hexha Northumberland).

Sorkin and Iamandi's previous book of poetry translation, *The Starry Womb* by Mihail Gălățanu, was published in 2014 in New Orleans by Diálogos Books.

Sorkin is Distinguished Professor of English Emeritus at the Penn State University, Brandywine campus.

Petru Iamandi, PhD, is an associate professor with the English Department of the Faculty of Letters, Dunărea de Jos University of Galați, Romania, and a member of the Romanian Writers' Union. He has written *American Culture for Democracy* (2001), *English and American Literature – Science Fiction* (2003), *American History and Civilization* (2004), *SF - Literature about the Future* (2004), *An Outline of American English* (2008), *An Introduction to Consecutive and Simultaneous Interpreting* (2010), *English for 14 Careers* (2011); edited *The Clock that Went Backward. An Anthology of Early American Science Fiction* (2010), *The Murder at the Duck Club. An Anthology of British and American Detective Stories* (2012), *The Voice in the Night. An Anthology of British and American Horror Stories* (2013), *Around the World in 80 Fairy Tales* (2015); and compiled an *English-Romanian Dictionary* (2000). He is the co-author and co-editor of several literary dictionaries and English textbooks.

Iamandi has translated more than one hundred books (prose, poetry, drama, non-fiction) from English into Romanian and Romanian into English, some of which have been published in the United States. Among the most prominent authors he has translated are Nobel Prize winners John Steinbeck, Nadine Gordimer and Harold Pinter, the Man Booker Prize winner Richard Flanagan, and the Women's Prize for Fiction winner A. M. Homes.

For the high quality of his translations, Iamandi has received a number of awards from the Romanian Writers' Union and various literary magazines.

Lightning Source UK Ltd.
Milton Keynes UK
UKHW011027260720
367198UK00001B/23